To Elaine McPherson,
God Bless you Always
from Donna

WARM MEMORIES AND SAD THOUGHTS

The author presents the reader with a very personal collection of her poems, expressing various aspects of her thoughts — both memorable and poignant.

WARM MEMORIES AND SAD THOUGHTS

Donna Campbell

ARTHUR H. STOCKWELL LTD.
Elms Court   Ilfracombe   Devon
Established 1898

©*Donna Campbell, 1998*
First published in Great Britain, 1998
All rights reserved.
*No part of this publication may be reproduced
or transmitted in any form or by any means,
electronic or mechanical, including photocopy,
recording, or any information storage and
retrieval system, without permission
in writing from the copyright holder.*

*British Library Cataloguing-in-Publication Data.
A catalogue record for this book is available
from the British Library.*

ISBN 0 7223 3179-7
*Printed in Great Britain by
Arthur H. Stockwell Ltd.
Elms Court   Ilfracombe
Devon*

Contents

For Our Princess — Late Diana	7
I Cry!	8
Dream Concluded	9
Reminiscing	10
Battered and Rejected	11.
Birds	12
Loving Our Saviour	13
War Zone	14
Flowers in Bloom	15
A Prayer!	16
The Ladies' Man!	17
Life as a Homeless	18
My Protector and Guide	19
An Ode to Those Who are Suffering	20
In Thy Name	21
Meeting Mr Right or Wrong	22
From Rags to Riches — From Riches to Rags	23
Voice of Experience	24
A God-Blessed Country	25
Thank You!	26
When I Think of You!	27
A Tribute to Princess Diana	28
A Beautiful Island	29
Our Love!	30
Forgiving God!	31
Life in the Sun!	32
Memories!	33
Nature at its Finest	34
Turning Point	35
I Walk with the Lord	36
One-in-a-Million Woman	37
The Delectable Lady	38
Love and Happiness	39
Oh Father	40
The Rain!	41
Sweet Sixteen	42
A Testimony	43
Mankind	44
With You	44
Wisdom!	45
For Dodi, Diana and the Princes	46
An Ode for George Michael	47
A Loving Prayer	48

For Our Princess — Late Diana

She was a God-Blessed Lady,
One with the utmost integrity.
She was a one-in-a-million woman,
The entire nation can most definitely understand.
She did so much for the whole world,
She never acted pretentious, neither was she cold.
She was a very warm loving lady,
She would hug the young, the old and the innocent baby.
Her kindness and tender loving care,
Deserves to be heard by everyone everywhere.
Her gift of life was so very special,
One that will be around in memory forever.
For she was a brilliant lady,
One with beautiful charisma and a wonderful personality.
With all the charity work that she did,
She was an exceptional lady who loved and adored the little kids.
Her life was cut short by an horrific tragedy;
I believe her soul will go to heaven,
Where she will live in paradise and happiness,
Where she most definitely deserves to be,
Because she was such a wonderful and caring princess;
So beautiful, so classic, she was such a wonderful success.
Her memory will most definitely live on,
Because in the eyes of everyone she was so special
And she made sure her work was superbly done.

I Cry!

Every tear that I cry,
The Lord will stand by,
Because I know He loves me;
He guides and blesses me.

His love is so warm,
Keeps me so calm.
I want the world to know,
Oh how I love Him so.

For He is a wonderful Redeemer,
A most glorious Saviour.
His guardian angels are guiding me,
They protect me and make me feel so free.
Sometimes I might feel sad,
The Lord makes me cheer up and feel glad.

For His love is so warm,
Keeps me so calm.
I want the world to know,
Oh how I love Him so.

The energy He gives me,
Is so warm and precious, I love Him so much.
I feel so courageously free,
That's because the Lord is guiding me.

The Lord's love for us will never die,
It's up to us not to change our minds.
For He has shown His love for us,
It's for us to show Him we love Him too,
The most glorious touch.

Dream Concluded

There you go once again,
And it's oh so very plain,
That you were the one who stole my heart,
Right from the start.

Dream now that you've answered me,
I will always love you;
No matter what we've been through,
I will always be loyal to you.

Now I can't afford to breakaway from you,
Cos I value our love which is oh so very true,
Because I've experienced once again;
You to me are more than just a friend.
It's fair enough for me to see,
What was once a dream, now appears like reality.

I am so pleased that it's you,
You were a vision that's come true,
And I'm so very proud,
That I can say it out loud.

Dream now that you've answered me,
I will always love you,
No matter what we've been through,
I will always remain loyal to you!!!

Reminiscing

Just sitting there all alone,
With no one to call their own.
Because they are getting on in age,
No one cares about them, it's such a terrible outrage.
They keep reminiscing on when they were young
And they would sing their favourite song.
Dancing right through the night,
Having a wild time and just feeling alright.
If only those days were here again
And they could have the chance to whisper each other's names.
Their memories are not the same as they used to be,
But they are getting there eventually.
They are a shadow of their young self,
But they loved each other and couldn't care for anything else.
In those days they knew about love,
And never treated each other rough.
Unlike the youngsters of today
They believed in love and would never stray.
If only we spare time and listen to them,
We would learn something again and again.
They have tales to tell which are true
And most of all, their love for each other,
Would always remain brand-new.

Battered and Rejected

They don't know what to do,
Unemployment has driven them to being cruel.
Day to day they rummage around in bins,
Quite naturally it's such a sin.
If only they could find
Something constructive to occupy their minds.
But they feel nobody really cares about them,
They keep thinking they're on their own
And things look pretty dim.
Just another statistic that's all they are
And all because they are so poor.
Poorness, poverty and crime, that's what they know,
But by giving them a chance, their confidence would grow.
We should look out for them and show them that we care,
Instead of treating them as if they're not there.
They are there for all eyes to see
So why don't we help them and let them feel free.
Because they feel like a prisoner for their situation,
It's not all their fault, they are a part of our nation.
So why don't we get together and do something about it,
Show them we care and that they really do exist!!!

Birds

Birds are wonderful creatures,
They are as beautiful as can be;
Their colours are so resplendent
For each and everyone of us to see.
When they sing, they make you very happy,
As cheerful as can be and happy-go-lucky.
Birds are wonderful creatures for you and I to see,
So beautiful sweet and nice, and as lovely as can be.
Especially in the mornings they give you a wake-up call,
To go to work each and everyone and all.
As they fly way up high in the sky,
They are such sensitive creatures, you cannot deny.
They come in all different shapes and sizes,
Even when they fly in the trees under heavy disguises.
Birds are beautiful creatures as can be,
So rare some types, but they are there for you and I to see.

Loving Our Saviour

Heavenly Father is a wonderful Saviour,
I love and worship Him — I'm a strong believer.
Loving Him is the best thing I can do,
He guides and protects me, I know He is true.
I have faith in Him and Him alone,
He always surrounds me, I'm never on my own.
He protects and blesses me day and night,
He makes me feel alright.
In everything that I do,
My faith carries me through.
I want everyone to know,
How I love the Lord so.
He is a wonderful Saviour — He is good to me,
He makes me feel so very happy.
There are times I might feel despondent and sad,
The Lord cheers me up and makes me feel glad;
I want the world to know,
Oh how I love Him so!!!

War Zone

The soldiers are wielding their weapons everywhere,
A little boy looks on and stares.
It's a heartbreaking situation,
Nation rising against nation.
People being used as human shields,
The soldiers look on, they feel pleased.
These innocent bodies just lying there,
Without no mercy, without a care.
The little boy looks on in disgust,
As he thinks this is human blood lust.
They are killing and torturing one another,
It's a crying shame on each other.
If only they could love one another,
Live in harmony and care for each other.
But the situation has gone too far,
It's war and bodies lying there, some in half.
This little boy is lucky to be alive,
As he creeps around a corner and hides.
He's lost his parents, he is all alone,
With no one to call his family, he is all on his own.
War is a language that a lot of people know,
Makes you wonder why they have to tread so low!!!

Flowers in Bloom

Violets are in bloom
In this spacious but empty room.
Busy Lizzies everywhere,
They are there without a care.
But they are pretty, they brighten up the room
And you'll see quite soon,
That the Joseph Coats are there
In many-splendoured colours for all eyes to see;
They're oh so pretty and radiant as can be.
Flowers brighten up the home,
Sometimes makes you feel you're not alone.
You can talk to them,
They can even be your friend.
But it's the way they grow that makes you know they're ok;
And when they bloom spectacularly, you will feel happy in some way.

A Prayer!

I know our Heavenly Father, He genuinely cares for me;
He always makes me feel so very happy.
When people try to persecute me,
He protects me, they cannot harm me.
Day and night His protective shield surrounds me.
That is why I have so much love and happiness for humanity.
At times I might feel ill,
I know His healing hands make me better, they always will.
I love our Heavenly Father so much,
The inner strength He gives me is warm and precious to the touch.

The Ladies' Man!

He was only forty-five years old;
Very mature and exceptionally bold.
He used to wear a ring on his third left finger;
The women loved him, for him they would linger.
He was a ladies' man;
I guess he is just your ordinary man.
He loved the ladies and how they loved him,
At times he felt like he was going around in a ring;
But he is ordinary like any other man.
I guess that's the only way he can understand.
He always promised them his love would be true,
And nothing could ever make him feel blue.
But he was deceptive in disguise;
Some of his ladies, they were wise,
Not to get too involved with him,
Because their lives would start looking pretty dim.
But he was very confident about himself;
Some would say selfish, he couldn't care for anything else.

Life as a Homeless

For quite awhile they have been homeless,
But they are trying their very best
To get their act together;
At times it seems pointless, it might take forever.
They are trying oh so desperately hard,
But their trying seems in vain,
It's like a never-ending task.
But perseverance is the name of the game;
Their life is in turmoil, it will never be the same.
For they are a victim of this society,
It's an on-going vicious circle, it's such a terrible tragedy.
But they are fearless, they will be on their feet one day;
Life in cardboard city, is what their lives portray.
At nights they are sleeping rough;
Life on the streets is very tough.
Sometimes they have to beg to survive,
Most times that's their only way to keep alive.
But they are sorry for their situation;
Together if we help them,
We would make a better and stronger generation,
For it affects their mental state;
Love for humanity is what we want to generate.
But it takes more than one to help them;
Together as a nation we could show them
We are not their enemy, we are their friend!!!

My Protector and Guide

I dream of the Lord as my protector and guide,
He is always on my mind.
With everything that I do,
My faith most definitely carries me through;
For I am a strong believer,
In my Lord and most wonderful Saviour.

For Jesus was born in Bethlehem;
He is more to us than just a friend.
He was born into this world to save mankind,
If we have faith and believe in Him,
We will be on His side.

For He loves us and He wants us to join Him,
In most glorious heaven where we cannot commit sin.
To drink milk and honey,
In His loving arms, is where we should be.

For Jesus was born in Bethlehem,
He means more to us than just a friend.
He was born into this world to save mankind,
If we have faith and believe in Him,
We will be on His side.

When we commit sin, the Lord will forgive us,
If we pray hard enough and worship Him so much.
For He loves us, we are all His beloved children,
All we have to do is trust, believe in Him and worship Him.

An Ode to Those Who are Suffering

Their bodies are just lying there cold, emaciated and callously bare;
They have been calculatingly killed,
God knows it's just a sin.
They have done nothing wrong,
But they are innocent victims of something they have not done.
It's horrific war and war alone
That tears apart a happy home.
Those who are lucky to be alive
Have to shelter, in haven they have to hide.
For they have lost their one and own,
And they are left cruel and bitterly, all alone.
The only happiness, the ones who are alive have
Is the small morsel of food that makes them feel glad.
The tiny portions keeps them just about alive;
Survival is what they are looking for,
Something they cannot hide.
But they are not sure what the next day is going to bring,
As each day passes, they feel that life looks pretty grim.
They are naked, not a piece of garment to wear,
Everyone together, just looks on and stares.
But they soon get used to being that way,
They hope that tomorrow will bring a brighter and hopeful day!!!

In Thy Name

In Your name Father, I put my trust,
With You most dearly in my heart,
For You are so good and wonderful to me,
I have You in my heart so tenderly.

For Heavenly Father gave His son,
To forgive our souls that we might live as one.
Because Jesus loves us,
In Him we should most definitely put our trust.

For loving You is the best thing we can do,
Towards us You are always so true.

For Father, in You alone I can express myself,
Because with You in my heart, I couldn't think of anyone else.
For You are our Supreme King,
Long may You reign respectfully.

In the eyes of everyone,
You are most definitely number one;
We love You and we know You love us.
The warmth and strength You give
Is most sensationally precious, very much!

Meeting Mr Right or Wrong

Her innocent-looking eyes glisten with sheer and utter delight,
At long last she is certain she has found her Mr Right.
His dark handsome smouldering looks,
Are reminiscent of a fictional character out of a romantic book.
He stares longingly into her sparkling green eyes.
"I love you", he whispers eagerly, to her surprise.
She ponders, this seems far too good to be true,
We've only just met,
It's a bit too soon to say "I love you".
He tells her reassuringly she's his fairy-tale princess,
And that out of all the ladies he has met
She is by far outstandingly the best!!!
She replies "I've heard it all before".
The truth is she loves it
And can't wait to hear a whole lot more.
He continues to compliment her on how lovely and stunning she is,
Then embraces her closely with a passionate, sizzling hot tender loving kiss;
She responds so tentatively to his warmth and exuding charm,
He promised her right from the start that he would make her happy
And never break her heart.
But hurting her is exactly what he did.
She was just another conquest on his hit list.
After convincing her with a whole pack of lies,
Along came the speedy exit and that was bye-bye!!!

From Rags to Riches – From Riches to Rags

He was only twenty-five years old,
With ambition and potential, he was rather bold.
He was a wealthy businessman,
One with charisma you can understand.
Some were optimistic, high-flying deals,
But surely only time would heal.
The dedication that he had,
Was inspirational but started to look gloomy and sad.
Because he was a good man,
One who set out to score a plan.
He was very ambitious, he thought everybody loved him,
They used to treat him as near as possible to a king.
But he was wrong and now he is sad,
While all his friends are laughing they all feel glad.
They were people who set out to rip him off,
He is now all alone, everything he once had now seems lost.
One thing he has is his pride,
No one can take that away from him,
No matter how hard they try.
But he is a man with ambition,
No matter what they do to him
He will come back with recognition.
Because he is a one-in-a-million man,
Whoever has let him down,
The problems they will face, they will never begin to stand,
For all the lies and deceitfulness and corrupt minds,
Destruction will face them and that is only a sign.
So let this be a lesson to one and all again,
Only God you can trust, but never trust a friend!!!

Voice of Experience

Voice of experience is a message;
To some people it might seem pretty average.
There is something I have to say,
And maybe some bright and cheerful day,
People might see and relate to me,
And their lives will transcend naturally.
It's all about people and nature;
Some would say it's more like an adventure;
But I know it's not necessary to shout,
I can only express myself out loud.
For writing about life is what I do,
Life in perspective, which is natural and true.
For in life people go through their ups and downs,
It's a regular occurrence when you're in this town.
But all you need to do to get through each day,
Is pray to Heavenly Father, He will guide you, and keep you,
With Him you will never fail.
So when you feel you are going through distress,
Tomorrow is another day,
Be optimistic, it might just bring you success.
So when you are facing a problem,
Pray to the Lord, He will help you solve them.
So this quite sums up what I have to say,
I hope when you read this, it might help in some way,
For encouraging words is what I have;
I never set out to make you unhappy,
Just to make you feel cheerful and glad.

A God-Blessed Country

England is a God-blessed country;
It's a safe haven for some of us to be,
Especially when we come from a foreign land,
The English they will understand.
Sometimes life abroad is pretty tough,
At times it can be very rough.
So if you feel you want a break,
Come to England and if you're ambitious,
A happy life you will make.
For a struggling life is where some of us are coming from,
But with patience and ambition, the Lord will make you very strong,
And you will find out in the long run,
That with life in this country, you cannot go wrong.
Especially in the summertime,
When you feel you need to unwind,
Escaping to the country or in the city,
Will make you so very happy,
That is when you realise England is the right place to be.
There are so many spectacular sights to see,
And the famous attractions shine so vividly.
So when you have some money in your pocket
And you have nothing to do,
Come to London Town and find out how life can become so true to you.
You will never regret a thing;
Love, laughter and happiness, is what London will bring!!!

Thank You!

Thank You Father for the life You have given us,
It's most gloriously wonderful as such.
The life You have given us is something to be grateful for,
Something so very special, we should most simply adore.

Father we thank You for Your precious time,
In the most glorious name of Christ,
Our Saviour and Redeemer;
Most of us are very strong believers,
For in You we put our trust alone,
Without You we would simply be on our own.

So Father thank You for being You,
You are so prestigious and true.
Without You a lot of us don't know where we would be,
Because You bring love, peace and happiness to us especially.

Thank You Father for health and strength,
For the breath of life.
In everything that we do,
Father, a lot of us are most sincerely true to You.

When I Think of You!

I remember sunny days in August,
We used to have so much fun together, just the two of us,
Visiting places we never frequently go;
But it was superb and I remember it so.

For when I think of you,
I think of happy days we used to have,
Fun and laughter, we were usually so happy and glad.

It's the fun times that I enjoyed best,
They most certainly beat out the rest.
It's most definitely *c'est la vie*,
Now we are both so carefree.

Reminiscing is what I am doing,
On the life that we were both once living.
We have grown apart somehow,
But wonderful memories is what I have now.

For when I think of you,
I am now feeling so blue.
I think of happy days we used to have,
Fun and laughter, we used to be so jolly
And now we are so sad.

A Tribute to Princess Diana

There are so many wonderful things to say about the princess,
That is why worldwide she was such a success.
She mixed and mingled with every nation,
She was such a beautiful sensation.
She was the people's princess,
She was beautifully elegant and so God blest,
For she didn't care where you originated from,
Her love for humanity is what she stood for
And she never did wrong.
Princess Diana was cheerfully respected by everyone;
Her memory will most definitely live on,
For Princess Diana did so much worldwide,
For every creed, colour, black and white.
She was a tremendous lady,
With warmth, compassion; she was a supreme lady.
Now our wonderful princess has gone,
Who is going to look out for us?
She was so warm and precious, very much,
For the world misses her so much;
The energy and strength she had is most precious to the touch.
Princess Diana represented peace, love and happiness,
She was most simply the best.
Princess Diana was very well-known worldwide,
Her brave courageousness is something special
That no one can take away from her
And they cannot hide.
For we all loved her and miss her terribly;
It's so painful she had to leave us
In such an awful tragedy.
The whole nation is in mourning,
For our beloved princess we are crying.
So what more can I say,
Except Princess Diana will be remembered in our lives day to day.
Rest in peace Princess Diana,
You will most affectionately live in our hearts forever and ever!!!

A Beautiful Island

Jamaica is a beautiful island,
Filled with fun and laughter throughout the land.
There are so many sights to see,
And the natives are so very polite and friendly.
The one thing you need to have,
Is money in your pocket which makes life cheerful and glad.
The food is nutritious, fresh and delightful,
When you eat, it makes you feel like your stomach is full.
But the tropical and fresh fruits are what I like best,
They are of the highest quality and so full of zest,
For Jamaica is the land I love;
Sometimes life might be pretty tough,
But you will find a tough life anywhere you go;
At times you might feel that life is a sad and pitiful no,
Nevertheless the natives will make you feel good;
All you have to do is travel around and take a good look,
For there are many splendid attractions to see;
The seaside, the tourist resorts, that will make you so very happy.
The scenery is for you to treasure,
It's wonderful and pretty, you can enjoy it at your own leisure.
Then when your time has come,
You have to wave goodbye to this beautiful island
And go back to where you originate from.
You've got the coconut trees swaying in the cool breeze,
As the temperature soars to over seventy degrees.
With the palm trees they are so ever green,
Nature is so wonderful, it's nice to be seen.
The sensational locations are just there,
They are in many-splendoured colours, everywhere.
So when you visit Jamaica for the first time,
You will be made so very welcome
And the service you will get, will most certainly blow your mind!!!

Our Love!

Sipping ice-cold champagne on a desert island with you,
Is most definitely something I would love to do.
I would most desirably like to fulfil my dreams,
With warmth, love and happiness, that reigns so supreme.

It's just like being with you,
That's the best thing I can do,
For you have made me so very happy;
I feel I'm a one-in-a-million girl, so happy-go-lucky.

For when I first met you,
We were like strangers in the night and so subdued,
But it's like since we've been together,
It feels like I've known you almost forever.

You've shown me you are so true,
It's a pity I didn't realise it when I first met you.
Nevertheless, you are so good to me,
Our love will always remain as special as can be.

Forgiving God!

Whenever you are feeling ill,
The Lord's healing hands will make you better, they always will.
For He knows your needs and your request —
He is most simply the best,
For He knows your trials and tribulations,
He is a wonderful Saviour towards His nation.

He loves us, that's why we must love Him,
That is why we should try so hard not to commit sin,
For He is our supreme leader,
Sent from above, He is a wonderful redeemer.

Lord please forgive us when we sin,
For we know You don't like those things.
You came into this world to save Your nation,
From which we should worship You with joy and elation.

The Lord knows our plight,
Even when we do wrong, He will forgive us;
We are precious to Him in His sight,
For He loves us much more than we will ever know,
Getting to know Him, will most definitely make us grow.

Life in the Sun!

On a sunny remote beach with you,
Is where I would like to be.
Where we could hold hands so casually,
And have a walk so leisurely by the sea.

Because we could look at the marvellous views,
Then just kiss and caress, just me and you.
This is something we would both enjoy,
Which would bring us total happiness and utter joy.

On the sun-soaked beach with you,
Where we could see all the clear colour views.
Dancing the night away,
Feeling total happiness, day by day.

This is my fantasy of being with you,
Where we could share such happiness which will one day come true.
If only we could live this dream forever,
Tomorrow is another day, one we can both treasure.
For we both understand,
What we have is very special and not underhand.

Walking barefoot in the sand,
Just the two of us, hand in hand;
Sipping cocktails in the sun,
And just having plenty of fun;
That's the way we should be,
Together forever, so tender and so gracefully.

Memories!

I was once with you so tenderly,
Now we are so distant, apart and so carefree,
For you have made me feel so neglected,
Worst of all, so bitterly rejected.

Tell me, where did we go wrong?
The way I feel, I don't know where I belong,
For I am so much mixed up;
It's because you are acting so abrupt.

My only wish is if only we could share good times,
But you seem to have a pre-occupied mind,
For you have bitter memories of the way we were,
While I reminisce on the way we used to confer.

For we were so good together,
Now we are apart, good memories I will treasure forever.
You will always be much dearly in my heart,
Even though we may seem so distant and so far apart.

So, tell me where did we go wrong?
Now I don't know where I belong,
For I am so much mixed up;
This is because you are acting so abrupt.

When we find out time is the master,
Let's just hope that we don't end up in disaster,
For when it comes to you time is what I have,
And when you think I've forgotten about you, by you I will stand.

Nature at its Finest

As the trees are whistling in the wind,
The birds display their happiness and sing.
It's a wonderful, spectacular sight to see,
While nature shines its light so evergreen.
This is nature at its best,
It's a natural existence, it beats out the rest;
For trees and birds are what we need,
They blend together, all you have to do is just wait and see;
Especially in the summertime,
They are a natural beauty in this time.
With the buttercups and tulips,
They are so brightly coloured, you cannot miss.
While the daffodils and the daisies,
They are so pretty amazing,
With shimmering colours that shine so bright,
They are a sight to see in nature's most finest lights.
Nature is a wonderful existence to have around you,
Somehow makes you so happy and you'll see you will never feel blue;
For trees, flowers and birds are so wonderful,
They are nature's finest beauties, so spectacularly beautiful.
So when you have nothing to do,
Study nature's finest beauties and see how they prove to be so true to you!!!

Turning Point

I've reached a turning point in my life,
Where things were once awkward, but now seems cheerful and bright.
My ambition was to score a goal,
But I have proved to one and all,
That I am onto a winner,
Even though at one stage in life I was just a beginner.
With everything that I do,
God is blessing me and I know He is true.
We all have to start somewhere in life,
Most of us at the bottom, then we will rise to glorious heights.
With all the mistakes I've made in the past,
Things are looking up for me, finally at last.
I've reached that turning point and life seems so pretty nice,
It only takes patience and understanding,
Which is oh so very right.
I remember starting out at first,
Then thinking things would only get worse,
But I was wrong and now I'm proud to say,
Everything is working my way.
So when you feel down in the dumps
And life feels pretty rough,
Hold your head up and say
Perhaps tomorrow will bring a brighter day.
It's plain for one and all to see
Ambition pays off, that can happen to one and all so naturally!

I Walk with the Lord

I walk with the Lord,
I talk with the Lord.
He is so very special in my heart,
He has been there right from the start.

Since I was very young and growing up,
I accepted the Lord as my Saviour
Which is a must;
For He died on the Cross,
To save us; He loved us a lot.

He still loves us and cares for us,
More than we will ever know,
So it's up to us to shine our light and forever glow.
In His presence this is a must,
For in our Good Lord, we put our trust.

He gives us hope when we cannot speak,
He lifts us up when we are weak.
He gives us strength to carry on,
He makes us feel that we belong.
You are my arms when I couldn't reach,
You are my destiny.
You are my guide, my everything,
He means the world to you and me.

One-in-a-Million Woman

He would climb the highest mountain,
He would swim the deepest sea,
He would do anything in his power,
To be with her endlessly.
For when he and her set up home together,
He vowed he would stand by her forever.
That is exactly what he has done,
She knows he is her number one.
She is most gloriously in the limelight,
She has risen to wonderful heights.
Her ambition is paying off,
That's because she's in a professional job.
What she does, a lot of women would like to do,
But not a lot of women have her standard figure, which is true,
For she is modelling.
Everything she does, she is just enjoying.
She is a one-in-a-million woman,
And she has found her right man.
Everything she does, he will stand right by her while he can,
For he knows she is his best bet;
She will be true to him and forget the rest.
Well she knows it's all in her best interest;
To have a man like him,
Is most definitely not a sin.
For they make a really good team,
What they've got together will make them reach to such prestigious esteem,
They are good for each other,
Their lives they will spend most happily together.

The Delectable Lady

She was almost irresistible;
Some would say most desirable.
It was awesome how she was loved by men;
They wanted her as more than just a friend.
That was not what she wanted,
She would never let them take her for granted,
For she was a lovely lady,
Even though she acted a bit crazy.
But that's what people loved about her,
She was always game for an adventure;
It seems she was a lucky star,
One who would most definitely get far,
For there's only one thing in this life you can do,
That will get you through,
And that is caring for yourself,
Putting your trust into God and no one else.
Self-preservation is what she's got,
It's better than the haves and the haves not.
She knows what she is doing,
And she's making sure no one is intruding;
For her men friends are nice,
But she's willing to let them bite the ice.
She is so very nice,
Nothing you can do will make her feel unkind.
She knows what she wants,
And will never put up with the awful taunts,
For that's exactly what she used to do,
Put up with people being so unkind and cruel.
But she doesn't have to do that any more,
For what she has she can simply adore.
She has made it to the top,
It will take a lot to put that at a stop.
She is big and you can't get any bigger,
All what she needs is for her own pleasure,
For she is a decent lady,
Even though she acted a bit crazy.
There is nothing that she can't almost do,
With her good attitude, it will get her through.

Love and Happiness

Life is like an adventure,
When you find out what you've been searching for,
Hope it meets up to the right measure.
For love and happiness are on the agenda,
When you find out hope, it gives you the utmost pleasure.
This is what a lot of people are searching for,
They hope that one day it will come knocking at their door.
But you have to go out and find it;
We all know that it naturally exists.
For love and happiness is a pleasure;
If you treat it right, you will never end up in danger.
Life is filled with happiness and joy,
All you have to do is not treat it as a toy;
Just appreciate what you have,
At the end of the day you will feel definitely glad.
Love and happiness are a natural existence,
All you must do is hope and never resist.
The temptation that love and happiness has,
Is something so very precious, it will never make you sad.

Oh Father

Father, You will help and guide us to eternal salvation,
For when we trust and believe in You,
You will save the whole nation.
Father, You are so wonderful,
Your gift of eternal life is so beautiful.

Because being with You is the best thing we can do,
Where everything we wish and pray for will come true;
For You are our only hope,
Without You Father, we would be all alone.

For You are my light when I couldn't see,
You are my everything to me.
You have my soul to keep,
You mean the world to me.
I've loved and lost not too long ago,
You have given me strength to carry on.
What would I do without You,
I would be sad, lonely and blue.

For God will supply our every need,
He knows that sometimes we are weak.
He will make us strong to go on,
To my dearest Father, I dedicate this song.

The Rain!

The rain is falling,
It feels like a storm is brewing,
For my heart is breaking;
It's all because of you.

It felt like we were together forever,
When in actual fact it was ten precious months to treasure;
So now that you are far away from me,
There is no need to feel selfish or angry.

So when the rain is still falling,
And the morning is dawning,
I would like to be with you,
Where everything we wish for will come true.

But I know it's just wishful thinking,
It's much better to live in hope where everything is succeeding.
I believe this will happen for us,
For the Lord above is in whom I put my trust!!!

Sweet Sixteen

She was only sixteen,
And was superbly hailed as the Caribbean Queen.
It all started at this young tender age,
Where everything she did was simply the rage.
She was a brilliant example to the youngsters,
They all treated her as a star,
For a star is just what she wanted to be;
She has made it at the age of sixteen.
Because she left school to fulfil her dream,
That was because she had ambition for everyone to see.
Now she is doing so very well,
It's a blessing and she knows it herself.
For she was very ambitious,
And she never acted pretentious.
Now she has made it to the top,
Her friends were soon getting jealous of her,
They want it to stop.
But there is nothing they can do,
For she has proved she can make it through,
Without the help of her friends;
She doesn't need them, she has her family
Which is a godsend.
Well she is doing what she does best,
And that is modelling with the rest
For they like her they know, she is good,
All they have to do, is just take a good look —
Especially like everything she has in her power
They know that she is onto a winner and is so remarkably clever.
She is doing well for herself,
All the media attention, she couldn't ask for anything else;
For she is a good kid.
No matter what, she will come through this, because she knows in her lifetime,
People might want to change her mind, from what she does best;
And that is moving among the rest.
She is now very much succeeding,
While her friends, they need convincing,
That she has come this far.
She is not a school kid any more, she is a star,
So let the moral of this story say,
When you are successful in life don't feel bitter or afraid;
For tomorrow is a brighter day;
Don't wait for things to happen, just do it and don't delay!!!

A Testimony

I believe in Your smile,
I know that it's worthwhile.
Every night and every day,
To You I will most sincerely pray.

For You are my symbol of peace,
You've helped me throughout my grief.
I know Father You will do this for all of us,
All we have to do is within You, we should put our trust.
For You were sent from above,
To bring us peace, happiness and love.
You mean the world to me,
Without You Father, I don't know where I would be.

Because You are so special Father,
Without You there would never be another.
For You are the magnitude in my life,
You help me through problems and strife.
Well You are so good to me,
My love for You is endless as can be.

Mankind

The way mankind are supposed to live,
Showing everyone that we truly exist,
Is the life we should have;
At the end of the day everyone would be glad.
For in our generation,
Some of us are trying to be a better nation.
But not all of us are like that,
Some of us are self-pitiful, gloomy and sad.
While we have the Lord on our side,
It's quite obvious we have nothing to hide.
Living in the most glorious harmony,
Is what we should do most naturally.
In our generation,
There should never be malicious hating,
For love is what we should have;
That will make life cheerful and glad.
Love is what I have in my heart,
It has been there right from the start.

With You

What I would most like to do,
Is bask in the sunshine with you,
Having loads of fun,
In the gloriously fine sun.
With you is where I'd like to be,
Living a good life tremendously;
Life can be full of fun,
When you find yourself with the right one.
Sipping a Tequila Sunrise,
This is most definitely the life.
If you can picture the scene,
You will know exactly what I mean.

Wisdom!

Father we ask You for knowledge and understanding,
So that we won't be too demanding,
For wisdom is what You give us;
It is very precious, so much.

For Father we thank You for everything,
The plants, the birds that sing.
Because on this earth You walked among men,
You know Father that a lot of us don't pretend.

To serve You most dearly,
From day to day, You are our energy.
We get the strength and love from You,
And with our faith it will carry us through.

For we believe in You,
No one could ever change our point of view.
We love You Father for who You are,
You shine so brightly like a star.

For love in our hearts is what we have for You,
To You Father we will be loyally true;
Because You mean everything to us.
If the world didn't have You, we would be at a loss.

For Dodi, Diana and the Princes

They made such a wonderful pair,
Even though they are both not here.
But they were good together,
Their love was a special one to treasure;
For they are so sadly missed,
I believe they are both in happiness and eternal bliss.
They will always be in our thoughts,
And most dearly in our hearts,
For they were taken so terribly from their families;
It's such an awful tragedy.
They were both unique individuals,
Who always treated everyone so civil,
For they were wonderful to the nation,
Whether it be the younger or older generation.
They were both warmly treasured,
So compassionate, their memories will live on forever.
Lady Diana loved and adored her sons,
They displayed their happiness as one,
For they were a very strong family,
What Diana's sons have to face is such an awful tragedy.
For the love from both sides was mutual;
This tragedy will be hard to face for the princes' future.
Diana loved and adored her sons and how they loved her;
In loving memory and God Bless her, is what they will both think of her!!!

An Ode for George Michael

I saw him in concert just a few years ago,
Unfortunately I couldn't get close to him to say a sincere, "hello".
He was dressed so immaculate like he always does,
The performance he gave made Earls Court really buzz!!!

On stage he comes across as someone so warm and full of fun,
He is a delight to see, he gives his all to please everyone.
In the eyes of many people he has a wonderful personality,
So full of joy, bubbly, he just shines most brilliantly.

He is so very loyal to his many fans,
The performance he gives in his concerts is one hundred per cent spectacular,
You can understand.
For he is most truly gifted,
With style, quality and charisma which makes one really lifted.

I don't know him personally,
In the public eye he is so natural and filled with integrity.
George is so very special to a lot of us,
His energy, his strength is brilliant so very much.

Not too long ago George has lost his beloved Mum,
Most endearingly precious, she was his superb Mum.
I can imagine now she is not here, he feels all alone;
Well it is nice to know he has his Dad and close family to call his own.

What would we do without our family?
They, with the spiritual help of our Dear Lord release us from our grief!!!
George, we are your most ardent fans;
Whatever you go through, we will be there for you because we understand!!!

There is one more thing I have to say,
George is respected by all his loyal fans in every way;
So no matter what,
We will stand by him a lot!!!

A Loving Prayer

Father, it's so nice to know You,
You represent our values, which are oh so true.
Because we live our lives,
To a standard which is high.

To meet Your most glorious requirements,
That's the way we want to be.
From up above Your son was sent to save us,
To save our souls and give us love.

For Jesus we know You died on the Cross,
To save us that we wouldn't go wrong.
You are a wonderful Saviour,
Within our hearts we love You as our Redeemer.

You've shown Your love which is true,
Now it's up to us to prove to You,
That we worship and love You day and night;
Without You dear Lord, we would be out of sight.

Your warm compassion is good to feel,
Your healing hands will always heal.
You are so good to everybody,
You mean everything to me.
You pick me up when I'm feeling down,
You put a smile on my face when there is a frown.
You are the best that there will ever be,
You bring me joy, that's why I feel so free.